Jane Goodall

Finding Hope in the Wilds of Africa

by Diana Briscoe

Reading Consultant:
Timothy Rasinski, Ph.D.
Professor of Reading Education
Kent State University

Content Consultant:
Sarah Baeckler
Coordinator
Chimpanzee Collaboratory
Washington, D.C.

Red Brick™ Learning

Published by Red Brick™ Learning
7825 Telegraph Road, Bloomington, Minnesota 55438
http://www.redbricklearning.com

Library of Congress Cataloging-in-Publication Data
Briscoe, Diana, 1949–
    Jane Goodall: finding hope in the wilds of Africa / by Diana Briscoe.
    p. cm.—(High five reading)
    Includes bibliographical references and index.
    ISBN 0-7368-3851-1 (soft cover)—ISBN 0-7368-3879-1 (hard cover)
    1. Goodall, Jane, 1934—Juvenile literature. 2. Primatologists—England—
Biography—Juvenile literature. 3. Chimpanzees—Tanzania—Gombe Stream
National Park—Juvenile literature. I. Title. II. Series.
QL31.G58B75 2004
590'.92—dc22
                                    2004003492

Created by Kent Publishing Services, Inc.
Executive Editor: Robbie Butler
Designed by Signature Design Group, Inc.
Edited by Jerry Ruff, Managing Editor, Red Brick™ Learning
Red Brick™ Learning Editorial Director: Mary Lindeen

Photo Credits:
Cover, page 28, KRT/Newscom; pages 4, 9, 15, 29, 31, 34 (bottom), 38, 50,
The Jane Goodall Institute; pages 7, 35 (bottom), Gallo Images/Corbis; page 13
(top) Brian Vikander, Corbis; page 13 (bottom), Bettmann/Corbis; pages 16, 20,
32, Kennan Ward, Corbis; pages 23, 24, 30, 35 (top), 42, 47, 48, 57, Michael
Nichols, National Geographic Society; pages 26, 33, 37, 41, 44, 45, Hugo van
Lawick, National Geographic Society; page 34 (top), Joe McDonald, Corbis;
page 52, Karl Ammann/Corbis; page 55, KRT/Newscom/People for the Ethical
Treatment of Animals

Printed in the United States of America.

2 3 4 5 6 09 08 07 06 05 04

Table of Contents

CHAPTER 1

Dreams

Are there things you dream of doing one day? Jane Goodall had dreams like that. She dreamed of watching and working with wild animals. She dreamed of learning things about animals that no one else knew.

When Jane first began watching chimps, she did it from a distance using binoculars and a telescope.

Amazing Discoveries

Jane Goodall had been observing chimpanzees for three months. She was in Tanganyika (tan-gah-NYEE-kah), now Tanzania, Africa. Jane was frustrated. The chimps would often flee as soon as they saw her. She tried not to scare them. Often she would watch them from a peak that looked out over the forest.

Then one day, a breakthrough happened. Jane met three chimps in the forest, and they did not run away! This was a turning point.

In the following weeks, Jane began to closely observe the lives of the chimps. She didn't know it at the time, but she was about to make some amazing discoveries. Her childhood dreams were about to come true!

---

observe: to study carefully
frustrate: to make someone feel helpless; discourage
flee: to run away from danger
breakthrough: a very important step in the progress of something

Getting to Know Them

As Jane was able to get closer to the chimps, she began to recognize particular ones. She gave these chimps names and began to identify their families. She saw how individual chimps interacted within families and within the whole group.

One day, Jane made an exciting discovery. She was watching a male chimp that she had named David Graybeard. He was eating something pink. Suddenly Jane realized what he was eating—it was meat! People had always thought chimps ate mostly plants and sometimes small bugs.

Three weeks later, Jane made an even bigger discovery.

---

interact: to act among or between others

Clever Chimp

Jane was watching David Graybeard again. This time he was with another chimp, named Goliath. The two were stripping leaves off twigs and using them to fish termites from a termite mound. They had made the twigs into tools! Before, people had thought only humans made tools.

This chimpanzee is using a twig to fish for termites.

---

termite: a small insect somewhat like an ant

An Early Love for Animals

How did Jane end up watching chimpanzees in an African jungle anyway? A look back at her life might show this isn't so surprising after all.

Jane was born in London, England, on April 3, 1934. For her second birthday, Jane's parents gave her a toy chimpanzee. The toy chimp was named Jubilee, after the first chimpanzee born at the London Zoo.

From a very early age, Jane was fascinated by animals. When she was 4, she hid for five hours in a henhouse to see how a hen laid her eggs. When Jane came home, she couldn't wait to tell what she had seen.

Jane's mother, Vanne, could see her daughter's excitement. "She noticed my shining eyes and sat down to listen to the story of how a hen lays an egg—the wonder of the moment when the egg finally fell to the ground," Jane later wrote in her book *Reason for Hope.*

---

fascinate: to attract and hold the attention of

Jane (on left) with her mother, Vanne. Jane always had encouragement from her mother, who told her, "If you really want something...never give up, you will somehow find a way."

Growing Up

In 1939, when Jane was five, the Goodall family moved to France. However, when World War II (1939–1945) started, they had to leave quickly. The Germans were invading France. The Goodalls would not be safe there. They took one of the last boats back to England.

Outdoor Girl

Jane spent as much time outdoors as she could. She studied the animals she found in her backyard. At age 11, she decided she wanted to visit Africa—maybe even live there. Her favorite books were the Dr. Dolittle stories and *Tarzan of the Apes.*

Jane finished high school. She still dreamed of going to Africa. Her mother suggested she go to school to become a secretary. Secretaries, Vanne told her, could find jobs anywhere! Jane took her advice and went to secretarial school in London.

secretary: a person whose work is keeping records, writing letters, and such for another person

Off to Africa

Jane next went to work for a university, and then for a film studio in England. Still, she wanted most to go to Africa. Finally, when Jane was 23, a friend in Kenya asked her to come for a visit. Jane didn't hesitate. She quit her job and bought a ticket for a passenger ship to Kenya.

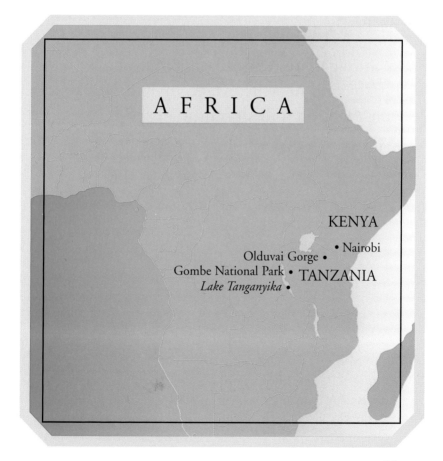

AFRICA

KENYA

• Nairobi

Olduvai Gorge •
Gombe National Park • TANZANIA
Lake Tanganyika •

Meeting the Leakeys

Jane got a job in Nairobi, the capital of Kenya. A friend there knew of her interest in animals. The friend suggested Jane meet Dr. Louis Leakey. Leakey was the curator of a natural history museum. Jane made such a good impression on him that Leakey offered her a job as his assistant.

At the museum, Jane learned a great deal about the wildlife of Kenya. The other staff encouraged her enthusiasm. Best of all, Leakey and his wife, Mary, invited Jane to join them on a fossil hunting expedition.

Each year, the Leakeys dug for fossils at Olduvai (OLE-du-vye) Gorge in the Serengeti (sair-en-GET-ee). The Serengeti is a region in Africa whose ecosystem has barely changed in the past million years.

---

curator: a person in charge of a museum
enthusiasm: a strong liking or interest
ecosystem: all the animals, plants, and bacteria living in a certain area

Olduvai Gorge in the Serengeti

Dr. Louis Leakey and his wife, Mary, examine fossils found while digging near Olduvai Gorge. Among their finds was a skull estimated to be 600,000 years old.

On the Plains of the Serengeti

When Jane went to Olduvai, the Serengeti had not yet been made into a game park. There were no roads or airstrips—just millions of animals.

Each day, Jane and the team descended into the hot, dry gorge. Jane crouched in the sun for hours, digging for fossils.

The fossils in the Olduvai Gorge are up to 3.5 million years old. Jane later wrote that she would "always remember the first time I held in my hand the bone of a creature that had walked the earth millions of years before."

Every evening, as she walked back to camp, Jane watched for wild animals. One night, she saw a rhinoceros. On another, she came within 40 feet (12 meters) of a young lion.

---

game: wild animals and birds
descend: to move down to a lower place
crouch: to stoop with the legs bent close to the ground

After three months, the group returned to Nairobi. Jane resumed her work in the museum. The fossil digging and museum work were interesting. But Jane still dreamed of working with living animals. That dream was about to come true.

Jane digging for fossils at Olduvai Gorge

CHAPTER 2

Into the Forest

Imagine traveling to a jungle or forest that you have never been to before. Would you be excited to explore it? Now imagine going there by yourself and staying for months. Would you still be excited to do it?

A village on the shore of Lake Tanganyika, Tanzania

A Challenge

One night, Louis Leakey talked to Jane about chimpanzees. He believed that if someone studied the way chimps behave, then that person would also learn how early humans had lived.

Leakey had found a group of chimps that lived near the shores of Lake Tanganyika. The land around the lake was steep, forest-covered hills. Leakey thought that it would be a good place to study chimps.

But Leakey warned that the location was far from any town. To watch the chimps, someone would have to spend years alone in the forest. It would take great patience and perseverance. He wanted Jane for the job. Jane was thrilled.

---

patience: the ability to put up with trouble, delay, and boredom without complaint
perseverance: the ability to continue doing something despite difficulty

All She Needed Was Money

Some scientists felt that Jane did not have the education to do good research. After all, Jane was not trained as a scientist. Leakey did not agree. He felt Jane would have new ideas about what she was seeing. She could watch and record what the chimps did. Then she could use this information to try to understand them better.

Jane and Leakey needed to raise money for Jane's research. They asked several groups for support. Since Jane had no college degree, however, most groups turned them down. At last, the Wilkie Foundation of Des Plaines, Illinois, agreed to help.

---

research: careful study to find out facts about something

Getting There

Jane made plans to go to Lake Tanganyika in 1960. The British government did not want a young woman alone in such a wild place, however. So Jane's mother, Vanne, went with her.

After some delays, the two women set off. First, they drove 800 miles (1287 kilometers) to Kigoma (key-GO-mah), a town near the Gombe Stream Chimpanzee Reserve. From there, they took a 12-mile (19-kilometer) boat ride to the reserve.

At first, the local Africans were worried. What were Jane and Vanne doing there? But they soon realized Jane wanted to study the chimps. Several guides and hunters taught Jane and Vanne bush lore. Then Jane's real work began.

reserve: land set apart for a special purpose
bush lore: knowledge about the wilderness handed down from earlier times

Settling In

The first three months at the reserve were rough. Jane had to keep her distance from the chimpanzees. The chimps did not trust her yet. Also, both Jane and Vanne became sick with malaria.

As the chimpanzees became more comfortable, Jane could observe them more closely. She made the surprising discoveries about them eating meat, and making and using tools. As years went by, she learned

more and more. However, some of what she learned about the chimpanzees was very disturbing.

This chimp dragged a baboon up into a tree so other chimps would not get her meal.

malaria: a disease caused from the bites of certain kinds of mosquitoes
disturbing: worrisome or upsetting

Not Always Lovable

Jane was shocked to learn that the adult male chimps hunted and killed monkeys for food. The males showed no pity for their prey. They tore the animals' bodies apart and shared them for food.

In 1974, the main group of chimps Jane was studying split into two. Over the next four years, the larger group waged war on the smaller group. In the end, the larger group killed all the males and three old females in the smaller group.

But Jane's worst moment came when she watched a female chimp named Passion capture and kill two baby chimps.

---

prey: an animal hunted for food by another animal

The Killings

Gilka, another female chimp from the same group as Passion, had a damaged wrist and hand. She had caught polio during an epidemic among the chimps.

Passion and her daughter, Pom, ambushed Gilka and took Gilka's baby, Otta. Passion killed Otta, then Passion and Pom ate the body. A year later, they did the same to Gilka's next baby.

Jane suspected that they had killed other chimps' babies as well. The killings stopped only when Passion and Pom had babies of their own.

---

polio: a disease which paralyzes parts of the body
epidemic: when a disease spreads rapidly through a population
ambush: to attack from a hidden place

Like Humans

Jane learned that chimpanzees behave like humans in many ways. If the chimps have not seen each other for a while, they may hold hands, hug, kiss, or pat each other in greeting.

Sometimes chimps behave like humans.

If they are frightened, chimps 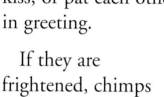 may hold onto each other, or run to find their mothers. Mothers play games with their children. Adult chimps may even tickle another adult or a young chimp.

Chimps spend a lot of time grooming each other. This is done not only to keep clean, but also to maintain friendly ties between family members and other chimps. Grooming can take place with several individuals and last for a few seconds, minutes, or hours.

---

groom: to brush and clean

23

This chimpanzee is communicating with other chimps.
Can you guess what the message might be by his expression?

Chimp Chatter

One main difference between humans and chimpanzees is that chimps can't talk. Their vocal tracts prevent chimps from being able to speak. Jane observed that chimps make lots of different noises, though. These noises give the other chimps information about things that are going on around them.

Chimps can probably recognize the sound of another chimp's call. This is like knowing which family member or friend is calling by recognizing the sound of his or her voice.

Listening and Observing

As a girl, Jane dreamed of talking with animals. Now, as a young woman, she had learned that listening and observing also could teach her a great deal. In the next chapter, find out more of what Jane learned about the lives of chimpanzees.

— CHAPTER **3** —

Life of a Chimp

"My favorite day is spent following a mother and her family until evening. The most wonderful thing about fieldwork, whether with chimps, baboons or any other wildlife, is waking up and asking yourself, 'What am I going to see today?'"

Jane Goodall studies chimpanzees from her tent.

Learning More

Jane began observing chimpanzees in 1960. Since then, she has learned a great deal about chimp life in the forest. For example, a chimpanzee in the wild can live to be about 50 years old. However, chimps are considered past their prime at around 33.

A baby chimp will ride underneath his mother, holding on to her belly, for about six months. Then, the chimp will mostly ride on her back for another two to three years. After that, the young chimp will walk and climb on his own.

A young chimpanzee will drink her mother's milk for the first three years. After that, the mother usually will have another baby. The young chimp then must find food on her own. For the next four to five years, the chimp will spend more and more time with other chimps her age. Together, the chimps discover the best feeding places and learn how to behave in the larger group.

---

prime: the best or most active period of life

Siblings

A young chimp is usually very interested
in a baby brother or sister. Sometimes
the older brother or sister is very possessive.
The older sibling might not let any other
chimps touch the baby.

A mother holds her baby chimp.

---

sibling: a sister or brother
possessive: showing a strong feeling for keeping something

Playtime

Young chimps will play games on their own. Chimps also practice tree-top gymnastics. This can be swinging around, doing somersaults, and jumping from high to low branches.

Young chimps also play games with each other, such as tag and wrestling. Sometimes they play with adult chimps, young and old tickling each other until both are laughing loudly.

Flo, a mother chimpanzee, plays with her baby Flint.

gymnastics: exercises that develop and train the body and muscles
somersault: turning the body forward or backward, head over heels

Not Just Fun and Games

Chimp games aren't only for fun, Jane learned. During their games, chimps learn about their playmates. They find out who is stronger or smarter. This is important because adult chimps live in a hierarchy. If a chimp is strong or clever, he may lead the group. If he is weak or different, other chimps may boss him around.

Many factors determine these rankings. Among them are the number of babies a female chimp has or how she interacts with the males in the group.

Chimps live in a hierarchy. Strong or clever chimps usually lead weaker ones.

hierarchy: any group in which there are higher and lower positions of power

Showing You Are Boss

Rankings are especially important for males. Males use "charging displays" to boost their status. During a charging display, a chimp first begins to rock from side to side. Then his hair stands on end. He makes pant-hoot sounds. These slowly get louder and louder. Finally, he leaps to his feet and charges at his rival.

During his charge, the chimp may throw stones. Or, he may drag a branch along the ground—a heavy branch that makes lots of noise is best!

A male during a charging display

status: position or rank in a group
rival: someone who tries to get the same thing as another

Friends Are Important

Jane also learned about friendship among chimps. Most male chimps have a special friend. Jane believes that this friend is often a brother. A chimp's special friend will help him if he is attacked. The friend will also back up a charging display.

Friends build their night nests close to each other. They feed together and spend hours grooming each other. If a chimp hears his friend call for help, the chimp will travel far to help him.

Two chimps groom each other.

Top Chimp

The higher a male chimp is ranked, the more females he can mate with. The chimp with the highest ranking is the alpha male. This chimp gets first choice of food and females, and everyone shows him respect.

A chimp can become the alpha male in two ways. He can defeat all the other males in fights, or he can frighten them into showing him respect with his charging displays.

One male Jane observed, named Mike, became the alpha male by frightening the others. He banged gas cans together during his charges to make them scarier.

Mike throws a gas can.

alpha: the strongest and most dominant

Read My Lips!

Jane also discovered that she could watch a chimp's face to tell how he was feeling. Here are some common chimpanzee expressions.

Relaxed

Playful

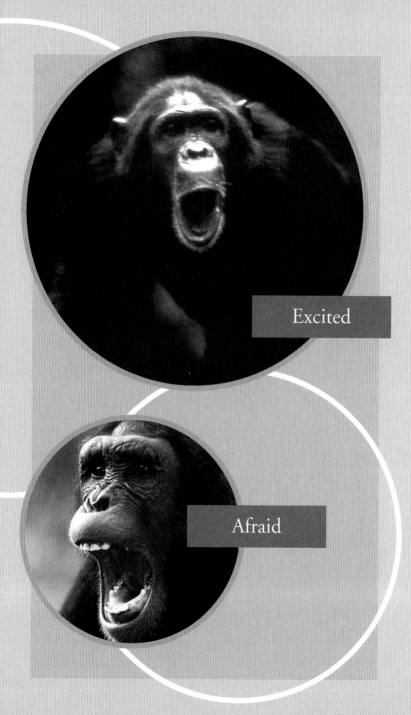

Excited

Afraid

Special Events

Jane observed how chimps respond to events in nature. She called one response the "rain dance."

Jane was watching a group of chimps when it began to rain. A flash of lightning was followed by a loud clap of thunder. Immediately, one of the large males began to move from foot to foot, almost as if he were dancing. Then he charged down the hill. Seeing this, two other males charged after the first chimp, breaking off and dragging large branches as they ran. Then a fourth male did the same. Others followed.

Jane observed this behavior during other rainstorms as well. The rain dances sometimes lasted for more than five minutes. Jane thinks the chimps may be challenging the rain and thunder, but she does not know for sure. What do you think of this explanation?

A chimpanzee performs a rain dance.

*Frodo in front of the waterfall
in Gombe*

Waterfall Display

There is a large waterfall at the Gombe Stream Game Reserve. Jane has observed male chimps swing on vines back and forth from one side of the waterfall to the other. Then they run and dance alongside the stream, throwing rocks into it. They repeat this for up to 10 minutes.

Jane thinks the chimps may be responding to the power of the water. In her book *Reason for Hope,* Jane wrote, "For ten minutes or more they may perform this magnificent 'dance.' Why? Is it not possible that the chimpanzees are responding to some feeling of awe? A feeling generated by the mystery of the water, always rushing past yet never going, always the same yet ever different."

---

awe: deep respect mixed with fear and wonder

Chimps and Humans

Scientists have found that human DNA and chimpanzee DNA are 98 percent the same. Some people argue that this shows a link between humans and chimpanzees. Other people disagree.

Louis Leakey thought studying chimpanzee behavior was important. He believed chimps could teach us about how early humans might have lived.

Jane went into the jungle to observe chimps firsthand. What she found often surprised her. She also grabbed the world's attention. Soon, others would join her in her research.

DNA: the material in a cell that contains the traits of a person or animal

Jane Goodall holds the hand of a young chimpanzee at Gombe National Park, Tanzania.

— CHAPTER **4** —

The World Takes Notice

When Jane Goodall began her work in Africa, other scientists didn't always respect her. For one thing, she hadn't gone to college. Still, she did keep good scientific records of her work. Also, she had made some pretty amazing discoveries about chimps! Over time, scientists and others began to listen to Jane. Maybe this young Englishwoman could teach the world something after all.

Jane carefully records her observations.

The Experts Listen

Jane had trained to be a secretary, not a scientist. Most scientists thought she could not do a real scientific study.

But Jane proved them wrong. She recorded her data properly so that others could check it. True, she wrote her reports more like stories than just facts. She also gave chimpanzees names instead of numbers. But she made some amazing discoveries, such as that chimps eat meat, and they make and use tools.

Jane wanted to continue her research, but research projects cost money. She needed another sponsor. The National Geographic Society (NGS) was very impressed with Jane's work. It said it would fund her work at Gombe for another year.

---

sponsor: a person or group that agrees to pay the expenses for another person or group
impress: to make people think highly of you

Jane Goes Back to School

Louis Leakey wanted Jane to be better accepted by other scientists. He arranged for her to study at Cambridge University in England. Jane went and earned a Ph.D. in ethology, the study of animal behavior in its natural environment.

In 1963, NGS sent a photographer to take pictures of Jane and her work at Gombe. His name was Hugo van Lawick. Like Jane, Hugo loved the forest and animals. He and Jane married in 1964 and had one son, Hugo, also known as Grub.

Jane with Hugo van Lawick, photographing chimps in Gombe

Ph.D.: the highest degree earned at a university

Banana Raiders

Jane's research center at Gombe was growing. She added two other staff members to assist her. In 1965, NGS paid for the construction of new buildings. The site included a special banana storehouse.

Jane had started feeding the chimps bananas in order to bring them closer and gain their trust. This caused some problems, however. Baboons raided the camp looking for the bananas. Chimpanzees raided the tents to do the same.

Jane experimented with "banana boxes." She found that the chimps would make tools from sticks to open the boxes.

---

raid: a sudden attack

Chimp Diet Test

Jane's husband joined in her work at Gombe. Hugo invented a way to find out what chimps had been eating. Called "dung swirling," this method was to wash chimp droppings and examine the remains of what the chimps had eaten.

Ethology students also came to help Jane at Gombe. These students knew nothing about the bush, so Jane sent an African guide with each one to watch the chimps in the forest. Some of the guides got interested and started to collect data as well.

dung: the waste matter dropped by animals
data: factual information about a topic

Jane spots a chimp for a student.

Speaking for Chimpanzees

Jane and Hugo divorced in 1972. In 1975, Jane married Tanzania's national parks director, Derek Bryceson.

From 1975 on, Jane began to spend less time at Gombe. NGS programs and articles about her work had made her famous. Jane began to travel and talk to many groups. She wanted to involve as many people as possible—particularly children—in understanding and protecting animals.

Jane talks with a group of students.

Teaching the World

Jane founded the Jane Goodall Institute for Wildlife Research, Education, and Conservation (JGI) in 1977. Its purpose is to support field research of chimpanzees.

JGI also supports other efforts to understand and protect the environment. Roots and Shoots is one of these efforts. Roots and Shoots involves students from preschool through college. This program supports students in projects that help people, animals, and the environment. There are 6,000 Roots and Shoots groups in all 50 U.S. states and nearly 90 countries worldwide.

---

institute: a school or organization for the special study of education, science, or art
conservation: the care and protection of natural resources
field research: observing animals and plants where they live

Recognition at Last

Over the years, Jane has received many honors for her work in science, and also for promoting nonviolence. Jane is a Commander of the British Empire, a high British honor presented to her by Queen Elizabeth II. The president of Tanzania awarded Jane the Kilimanjaro Medal. She is the only person who is not a citizen of Tanzania to receive it.

In 2002, Jane was named as a United Nations Messenger of Peace. Jane received this honor for her work in science.

---

nonviolence: the practice of using peaceful means to solve problems

On the Road

Today, Jane travels around the world to speak about the environment and Roots and Shoots.

Jane only manages to visit Gombe for a few weeks each year. But those weeks are precious. As Jane says, "I think a forest is really my spiritual home. So, when I came to Gombe, I really was home. It's a world that doesn't change in a world of change. It's my spiritual anchor."

Alongside her work with Roots and Shoots, Jane has created programs to help chimps all over the world. Read on to find out more about how Jane helps chimps everywhere.

Jane receives the United Nations Messenger of Peace Award from Kofi Annan.

precious: much loved; having a high value
spiritual: having to do with religion; sacred
anchor: anything that keeps something steady or firm

— CHAPTER **5** —

Helping Chimps Everywhere

Jane believes that every person makes a difference every day. That is one reason why she spends so much time traveling and speaking to groups of people about the animals, forests, and people she loves. She believes no person is too small to make changes in the world. Do you agree?

Jane photographs two chimps grooming each other.

Chimp Sanctuaries

The Jane Goodall Institute works with chimpanzee sanctuaries in different parts of Africa. Orphaned chimps live in the sanctuaries, where they enjoy some freedom. Caring, trained keepers look after them.

The sanctuaries' staff hire local people as keepers, guards, and teachers. They buy fruit and vegetables from local vendors to feed the chimps. They try to include the local community in the effort to save the chimps.

Help for Local People, Too

At one sanctuary, the JGI is building a small health center for the nearby villagers. Each sanctuary has an education center to help the local people, especially the children, learn more about chimps.

---

sanctuary: a place where animals are protected
orphaned: being a child whose parents are dead
vendor: a person or business that sells goods

ChimpanZoo

Jane founded ChimpanZoo in 1984. This research program studies apes in zoos around the world.

The goals of the ChimpanZoo project are to:

- increase public awareness and understanding of chimpanzee behavior;

- assist zoos in efforts to improve conditions for captive chimpanzees;

- help share information on ways to enrich the lives of captive chimpanzees.

The zoos and JGI train students and other volunteers to record the captive chimps' behavior. They then compare this with the behavior of chimpanzees in the wild. The students also work with zookeepers to improve the lives of chimpanzees in zoos everywhere.

---

ape: a large animal related to a monkey, but with no tail

Stop Research That Harms

Jane also campaigns against using chimps in medical research. She believes that scientists should move away from doing research that harms animals. She feels there are other ways to gain the information scientists are looking for.

This chimp is being held in a cage for medical research.

campaign: to take part in a series of actions for getting something done

Bushmeat

Jane also has been telling the world about bushmeat. She says, "The bushmeat trade is commercial hunting—hunters going from the city to the end of the logging trails, shooting everything, loading it on trucks and taking it to the city, where it fetches more money than domestic animal meat. Bushmeat is a delicacy. It's not used to feed starving people."

More than 2,000 hunters shoot more than 4,000 chimps illegally each year. That's 20 times the number of chimps who live near Gombe Stream Game Reserve.

Founded in 1996, the American Bushmeat Project tries to get people to stop eating bushmeat. It also shows local people why live apes are more valuable to them than dead ones. The JGI and many other organizations provide support for this project.

---

bushmeat: wild animals killed and sold for food
commercial: having to do with making money
delicacy: choice or special food

Follow Your Dreams

Through her work with chimpanzees, Jane Goodall hopes to inspire children everywhere. She hopes to encourage them to do the right thing—to respect one other, to work hard, and to follow their dreams. Jane did—and look where her dreams took her.

Jane with her first chimpanzee, a doll named Jubilee

Epilogue

Danger Ahead

The research and discoveries of Jane Goodall have taught the world amazing things about the lives of chimpanzees. But her work has also shown the many dangers that chimps face.

Chimpanzees are losing out to the ever-growing needs and desires of people. People have exploited the land where chimps live. War has also destroyed chimpanzees and their habitat.

In 1900, between 1 and 2 million chimpanzees lived in Africa. Now only around 150,000 are living in the wild. It is estimated that only 8 percent of chimpanzees' current habitat will be left untouched by the year 2030.

---

exploit: to use in a selfish way
habitat: the place where an animal or plant is normally found

Hope Ahead

Still, Jane is hopeful about the future. In a book she wrote titled *Reason for Hope*, Jane states that people have begun to understand and face up to the world's problems. She believes there is growing energy from young people around the world to make changes. Also, many people have dreamed and achieved amazing things, Jane writes. This has inspired others to dream and achieve difficult goals.

Jane Goodall has taught the world much more than facts about chimpanzees. She has taught people to care about each other and their environment. She has inspired people to have hope and to become caregivers of the future. Are you one of those people?

caregiver: a person who gives care to something

Glossary

alpha: the strongest and most dominant
ambush: to attack from a hidden place
anchor: anything that keeps something steady or firm
ape: a large animal related to a monkey, but with no tail
awe: deep respect mixed with fear and wonder
breakthrough: a very important step in the progress of something
bush lore: knowledge about the wilderness handed down from earlier times
bushmeat: wild animals killed and sold for food
campaign: to take part in a series of actions for getting something done
caregiver: a person who gives care to something
commercial: having to do with making money
conservation: the care and protection of natural resources
crouch: to stoop with the legs bent close to the ground
curator: a person in charge of a museum
data: factual information about a topic
delicacy: choice or special food
descend: to move down to a lower place
disturbing: worrisome or upsetting
DNA: the material in a cell that contains the traits of a person or animal
dung: the waste matter dropped by animals
ecosystem: all the animals, plants, and bacteria living in a certain area
enthusiasm: a strong liking or interest
epidemic: when a disease spreads rapidly through a population
exploit: to use in a selfish way
fascinate: to attract and hold the attention of
field research: observing animals and plants where they live
flee: to run away from danger
frustrate: to make someone feel helpless; discourage
game: wild animals and birds
groom: to brush and clean
gymnastics: exercises that develop and train the body and muscles
habitat: the place where an animal or plant is normally found

hierarchy: any group in which there are higher and lower positions of power

impress: to make people think highly of you

institute: a school or organization for the special study of education, science, or art

interact: to act among or between others

malaria: a disease caused from the bites of certain kinds of mosquitoes

nonviolence: the practice of using peaceful means to solve problems

observe: to study carefully

orphaned: being a child whose parents are dead

patience: the ability to put up with trouble, delay, and boredom without complaint

perseverance: the ability to continue doing something despite difficulty

Ph.D.: the highest degree earned at a university

polio: a disease which paralyzes parts of the body

possessive: showing a strong feeling for keeping something

precious: much loved; having a high value

prey: an animal hunted for food by another animal

prime: the best or most active period of life

raid: a sudden attack

research: careful study to find out facts about something

reserve: land set apart for a special purpose

rival: someone who tries to get the same thing as another

sanctuary: a place where animals are protected

secretary: a person whose work is keeping records, writing letters, and such for another person

sibling: a sister or brother

somersault: turning the body forward or backward, head over heels

spiritual: having to do with religion; sacred

sponsor: a person or group that agrees to pay the expenses for another person or group

status: position or rank in a group

termite: a small insect somewhat like an ant

vendor: a person or business that sells goods

Bibliography

Goodall, Jane. *The Chimpanzees I Love: Saving Their World and Ours.* New York: Scholastic, 2001.

Goodall, Jane. *Through a Window: My Thirty Years With the Chimpanzees of Gombe.* New York: Houghton Mifflin, 1990.

Maynard, Thane. *Primates: Apes, Monkeys, and Prosimians.* A Cincinnati Zoo Book. Danbury, Conn.: Franklin Watts, 1999.

Meachum, Virginia. *Jane Goodall: Protector of Chimpanzees.* People to Know. Springfield, N.J.: Enslow Publishers, Inc., 1997.

Useful Addresses

The Biosynergy Institute (Bushmeat Project)
P.O. Box 488
Hermosa Beach, CA 90254

The Jane Goodall Institute (U.S.)
8700 Georgia Ave, Suite 500
Silver Spring, MD 20910-3605

The National Zoo (Friends of the National Zoo)
3001 Connecticut Ave. NW
Washington, D.C. 20008

Internet Sites

Discover Chimpanzees: Jane Goodall Institute's Center for Primate Studies
http://www.discoverchimpanzees.org/researchers/center.php

National Geographic: Jane Goodall
http://www.nationalgeographic.com/council/eir/bio_goodall.html

The Jane Goodall Institute
http://www.janegoodall.org

Index